1.50

This book is dedicated
to
minding my P's and Q's.

I'm Abe, and it's time for me to move.
A letter adventure awaits, and I approve!

Through the ABC's we'll hike,
Finding letter shapes we like.

A is for Arrowhead.
It has a sharp tip.

B is for Butterfly.
It loves to fly
and dip.

C is for Caterpillar curling to eat.

D is for Dust pan and keeping things neat.

E is for Elephant.
What a big sneeze!

F

is for Flag flapping in the breeze.

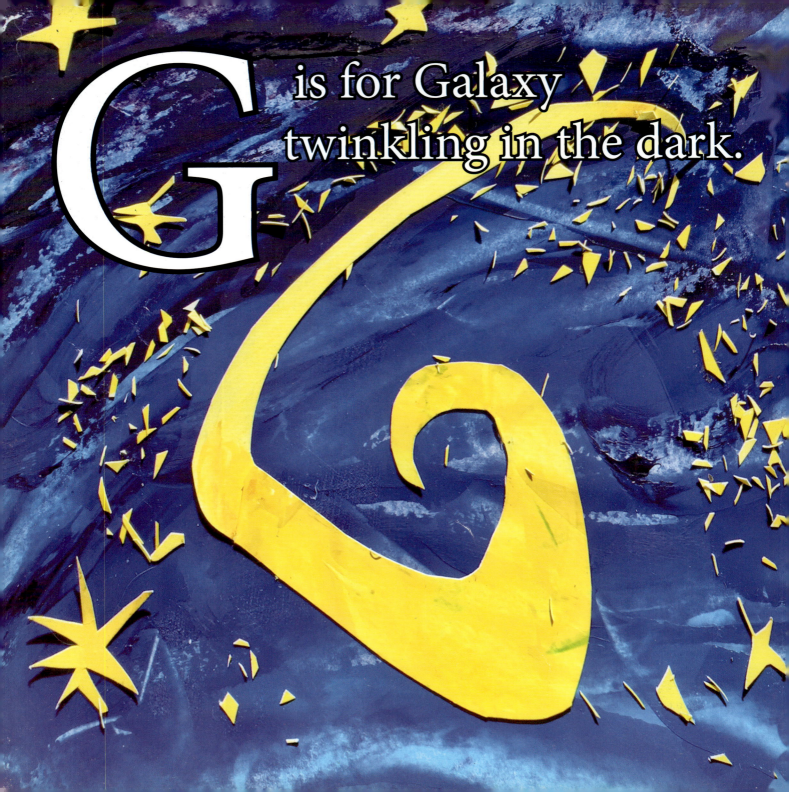

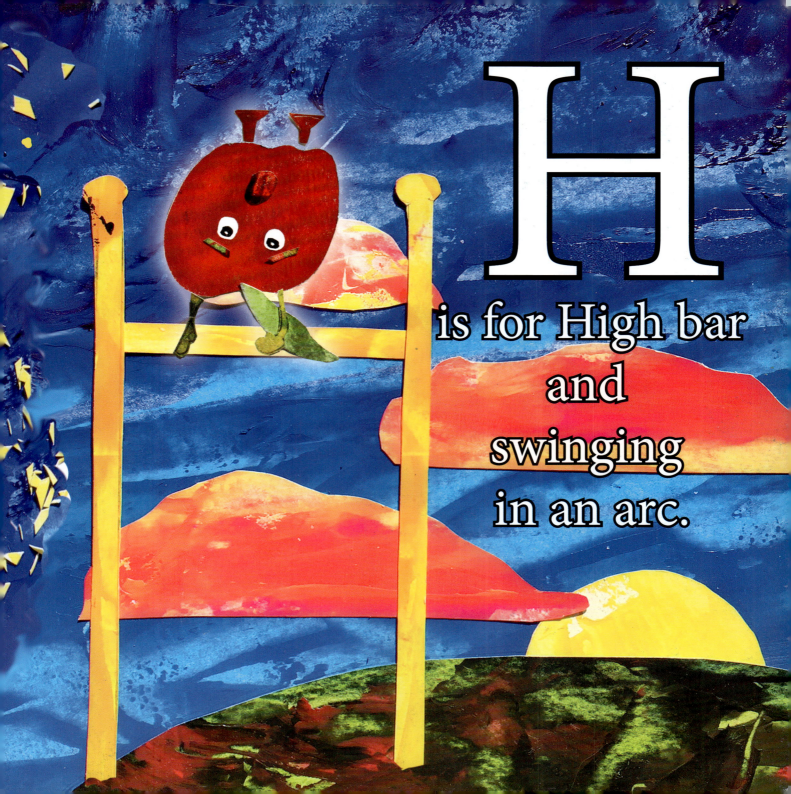

I is for I-beam. They make buildings strong.

J is for Jig and fishing all day long!

K is for Karate.
We will kick and bow.

L is for Left. Your fingers show you how.

M is for Mountain. It's a long hike to the crest.

N is for Nothing, because I need a rest.

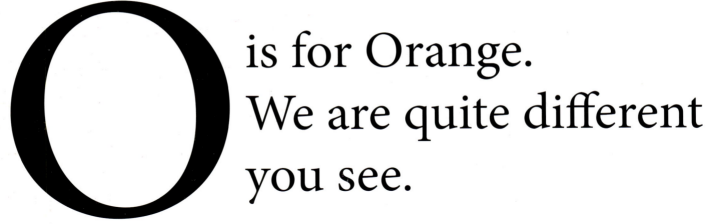

O is for Orange.
We are quite different you see.

P is for Piano and fingers tickling the keys.

Q is for Quail hiding on the ground.

R is for Ribbon curling all around.

T is for Tack.
Hammer it with might!

U is for Umbrella tipped the wrong way.

V is for Vase. A place for flowers to stay.

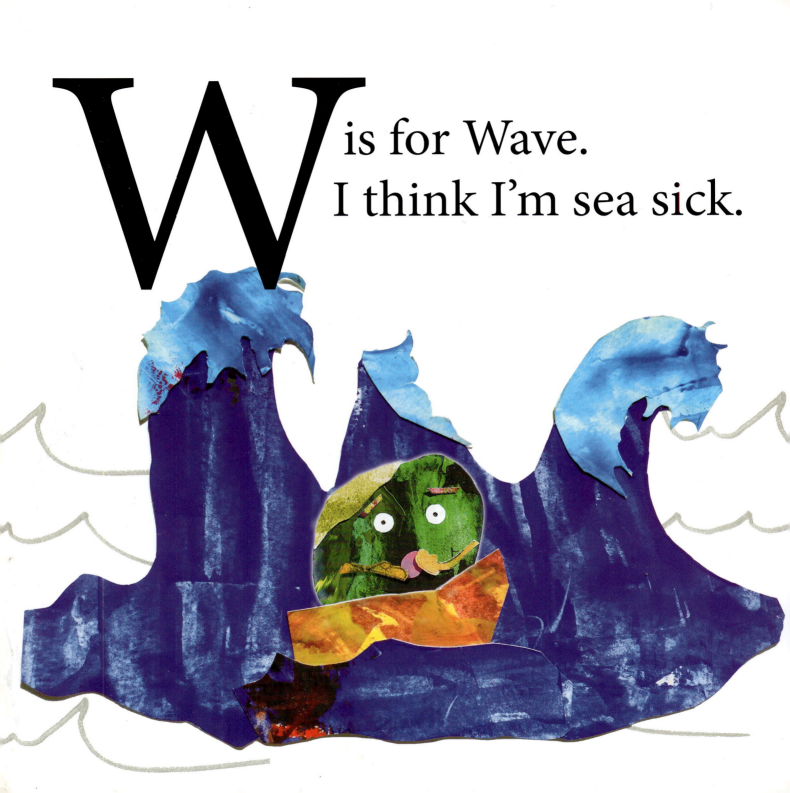

W is for Wave.
I think I'm sea sick.

X is for Xylophone with its special sticks.

Y is for Yoga. It makes you feel strong and light.

Z is for Zigzag with its sharp lefts and rights.

My friend, here we are at the last page.
But you are of an early learning age.

So read the book again and linger,
Tracing letter shapes with your finger.